EVERYTHING IS MESSY

A book about resilience, reality, and personal development

with recipes to help you live a

happy, healthy, positive, and productive life.

Stories. Solutions. Mindset. Meals.

It is time to get organized, put in the work,

and turn your dreams into a reality…

KELLY ANN GORMAN

ISBN: 978-0-578-77662-0

Library of Congress Control Number: 2020947666

First paperback edition November 2020.

Printed in the United States of America

A MILLION
DREAMS
PUBLISHING

If you are unable to order this book from your local bookseller,
you may order directly from the publisher.

amilliondreamspublishing.com

Jessica

"DREAMING, AFTER ALL,

IS A FORM OF PLANNING."

GLORIA STEINEM

I hope you enjoy
this book and all
the recipes!

Kelly
Ann
Gorman

CONTENTS

INTRODUCTION

You are reading this book right now because you want to get organized, grow as a person, figure out your purpose in life, start the business of your dreams, or up-level the one you have now. You are also in the market to learn how to create some delicious new meals. Budget-friendly vegan meals with no meat, dairy, gluten, sugar, or BS. However, you can always add those when you feel necessary. Without the BS, of course, because we are keeping it real here. I will have all my recipes listed for you throughout this book. Breakfast, lunch, and dinner, as well as some savory sides and nightcaps for the sweet tooth. I want you to get creative and make them your own. I want you to take the time and always come back to the book when you need it.

Listen, everyone has a story to share, and this is mine. A happy one. A healing one and a humorous one. We have all had crazy life experiences. Some of us take the lessons from them and move on, some turn it into a business, and some turn it into a purpose behind the drive to helping others.

I want to share a few quick things with you now, so there is no confusion. I am not an expert, I am not a Vegan (I just eat like one most of the time), and by no way, shape, or form am I normal. I have never been. So why should my business or book be any different? Throughout this one of a kind personal development/cookbook, you will receive all the tools and ingredients you will need to do what I mentioned above. Make amazing healthy food while taking your life to that next level you deserve to be at. I am giving you all the recipes to make them a success.

I am quite sure that you can pick out one thing in life that you are trying to heal from. Throughout this book, there will be chapters that will really make you think, and I am not just talking about measurements because the collection of recipes in this book have all been filed under a category I like to call common sense cooking.

I want you to be able to take everything I share with you here and implement it into your world immediately. Life is short, so take the steps and do the work now.

You have got to get your thoughts and mind together before you put in the work, and that is what each chapter is about.

Now a little bit about me so that you know where you are getting this incredible information from. Someone with a lot of experience. And I mean a lot.

Ever since I was little, I was always creating something. I remember cutting coral sponges to paint my room in pastels. I remember drawing out a floor plan to reorganize my room every other month and in my 20s, designing the floor plan for my one-day future restaurant. I have even created jobs that did not exist. Traveling the world on cruise ships, yachts, and private planes to my own podcasting and luxury experience companies. When I say anything is possible, these are just a few examples.

Putting in the work is something you are going to have to get used to if you want to grow as a human. I know this because I have been doing it for years, and it has gotten me to a great place today.

You've got to learn how to calm your own mind and thoughts, get scheduled, organized, and create a routine that works best for you. One that you truly enjoy, or this whole personal development thing you are trying to do won't work.

I believe in doing anything your little heart desires. You want more than one thing in life? You can absolutely have it! Go and chase those dreams but remember to be smart about it. Don't listen to anyone else because their opinions don't matter here. Again, organized, scheduled, and here comes that routine again.

What to expect from this book...

Personal development, life lessons, true stories, healthy recipes, and proof that anything is possible when following the right formula. A lot of my happiest times have been spent in the kitchen. A place that has helped me heal. Mentally, physically and emotionally. I've also laughed and cried a number of times, usually over a failed recipe, but when your friends are gathered around a good dish, what could go wrong? Friendly reminder here; if you ever fail in the kitchen, laughter is always the best medicine. No stress allowed over here...

I want you to enjoy this journey. I want it to really make you think about the serious shit you have going on in your life. The goals you have and the dreams you stopped chasing. I want this book to help you level up in the kitchen, and I want it to make you dream and believe again in your life. I want it to make you stop complaining, blaming others, and living in a negative mindset. That all stops today if you want any of this to work out for you.

You can, and I promise, have anything out of life, but you simply must put in the work. Use this book when you need it. Come back to it and, of course, share it with a friend. It is better to go through these times in life with an excellent support system, a good head on your shoulders, a sense of humor, and the understanding that manifesting can change your life, but it's when you start to visualize the outcome and acting as if it's already here that it actually happens for you.

If you have a family to worry about every day or it is only you, that is okay. Even if you have a team surrounding you, you can still feel alone (trust me, that was me for many years). The good news is now you have me as well as the community surrounding this book. The happiness, laughter, and joy will come again, if that is something you are currently searching for. I found it, and now it is my purpose to show you how to get it, chase it, and make everything you want to become a reality. You must be hungry! There is no half-assing allowed here.

Now let's get this party started…

CHAPTER ONE

GET ORGANIZED

Today is the day to stop making excuses. We all know that there is not enough time in one day to do everything we have on our to-do lists. That is why you wake up earlier. If you get up a little earlier, then boom, those are the extra hours you've been searching for. See, I wasn't kidding about putting in the work. That's all I did to get me to where I am today, and quite honestly, it's why you are here. You were curious. And in your subconscious mind, you are all ready to do more today. To be more.

It's why you picked up this book. You are ready. You know it. You can feel it, and you just needed that extra push, so here I am. I just want you to know that I will be your biggest cheerleader throughout our time together. I know you can crush your goals. Again, I am not an expert; I am just following a highly successful formula.

The first step is to get organized. Like I mentioned earlier, your mind, thoughts, home, office, kitchen, busy brain; all of it. Find the time to make a list of everything you want to accomplish, put together a schedule, and create achievable goals.

My routines (especially morning) have made the biggest difference in my life. I start with a gratitude practice. Meditations, sound baths, repeating my favorite affirmations, and breathwork. I wake up and make my iced coffee. I sip slowly (I try) so that I can thoroughly enjoy it throughout this morning ritual I have created for myself. My evening ritual may include some movie watching, book reading, a hot salt and essential oil bath, or just some white noise, healing music, or meditations to go to sleep. It absolutely includes my crystal-filled weighted blanket, as that has been a game changer for my sleeping and anxiety. The best pandemic purchase yet.

All my rituals, whether morning or night, will change depending on my mood, and that is perfectly okay as they are my rituals. Yours will also look different, and that is the best part about getting creative and tapping into your intuition.

I've always been a super organized person. I'm fully aware of how that may not come so easily to you. But again, that is why you are here. I want to keep everything in this book as simple as possible. Basics! I want to set you up for success, so let me tell you what you are going to need.

A notebook, sticky notes, a highlighter, pens, pencils, a cozy little area just for you, whatever is going to make you feel good right now. If you are not prepared, make a list now and come back to me. I love the note section on my phone. I literally have thousands of them saved. As soon as I think of something, it gets put in there. So many ideas and recipes for this book you are reading right now started there. If you are here for growth, use this book as somewhat of a journal prompt. There are going to be some hard projects to tackle throughout our time together, but so many that will come much easier than you ever knew possible.

It's just that you've chosen to take this path now. I'm a huge "use what you have" supporter. That's honestly how I came up with some of my best recipes and business courses. The purpose of this book is to help you heal and grow, not to spend money. So, go to the damn dollar store if that's the kind of budget that you're rocking with these days. Aghh, the dollar store. I love that place, and I'm telling you, all you need is a writing utensil at the very least so that you can write all over this book.

This will be your number one tool to help you up-level and create the happy, healthy, positive, and productive life you're currently craving. And by the way, you are so deserving of it. We all are. Isn't writing in books the best? Just make this your own. Own all the feelings here!

Now that you know what you need and how to start this process, I want to get into the gritty part of getting organized. I'm a huge planner, always have been. It's such a good trait to have. An even better one would be to know how to roll when shit on your list doesn't get checked off, a wrench gets thrown into your day. That took some work for me as I am hands down a perfectionist and borderline OCD, but in a good way, you know...

Is your kitchen clean? Let's start there. What do you need to do to get it the way you want? I'm guessing you can throw a lot of stuff away. If you can give it away, obviously do that. Only have what you use out and readily available. Store everything else away. This is where my professional organizing advice comes in. Use what you have, old shoeboxes, unmatched Tupperware, new finds from the dollar store, and put everything you need directly in front of you. Anything clear and/or open so you can see it.

When I made the decision for this personal development book and cookbook to join forces, I started to search for a little pantry to have in my room so that from the moment I wake up, I am immediately inspired. I saw my cute little dresser I purchased from an app for $50 and started to organize everything I wanted in there. What dry ingredients, cans, boxed goods, and cooking utensils made the most sense. This is what you need to do. Start to get inspired.

I also have six rectangular-shaped bins that hold my spices and other dry goods that are arranged by shape and if they are for baking and cooking. Keep it simple. Find a cute little space for you to makeover if you don't have one. Create the space, go through cabinets, and clear out the shit that is no longer serving you. I'm telling you, it feels incredible! Put together everything you use daily, and then let's do the same with your fridge and freezer. I'm a big meal prepper and use plastic bags and storage containers to allow more space. I also reuse and wash everything. No single uses over here! I would love to tell you that I am a minimalist, but I'm not 100% there. Maybe by my next book. However, I have slowly transitioned over to glass, so please don't come after me because of the plastic.

When it comes to cooking, I want you to enjoy the process of using the ingredients you already have. Use those damn leftovers. Think about what you have in your refrigerator right now. Can you maybe add one or two more ingredients to make it a whole new meal? I bet you could if you had an organized pantry and freezer already.

Everything has a shelf life, so when you start this cleaning out, please check those dates and again throw away what is not going to work. I want to share a great tip with you. I do this in my office and in the kitchen at night. Everything must be clean and put away. For example, my planner and notebooks must always be closed at the end of the night with the next day already planned out. This way, when I wake up, I'm starting the day on a clean, fresh slate. Every day is a new beginning and another 24 hours that allows you to chase those dreams.

I meal prep for two reasons. One, because I love the organization aspect of it. Two, it keeps me on track when it comes to eating healthy. I'll be honest; when I'm at my computer, I could easily put in a six-hour day without even getting up. Not even to go to the bathroom. I know, it's such a terrible habit…

When I meal prep, everything is done the night before, usually a few days. My green juice and protein shakes, lunch, and dinner options are already prepared and ready to go. If I crave something different and have the time, then I make that. Again, always have a few varieties ready to go!

I have several friends that hate freezing meals or blending juice and shakes two days ahead. Listen, I'm just sharing what works for me. I know my recipes last, and when you make them, follow my directions, and you will agree. I love a good mason jar. Small, medium, and large. All the sizes. I use these to keep my juices, milks, and protein shakes fresh.

They will stay for up to three days. The fourth is really pushing it. When it comes to meals, I have a few tricks. Obviously, the containers to hold individually prepped meals. This trick is also a great idea for kids learning how to feed themselves with healthy treats. Especially on the days that they open the fridge 500 times a day looking for something. Show them the system. Have them write their names on them or set alarms. Kids are smart; they'll figure it out in a day. If you have a meal you want to eat every day, then keep it in the fridge. Backups can be frozen. Sometimes, rather than prepping individual meals, I just prep each ingredient separately, so if I decide to create something else with it, I'm not wasting. For example, sautéed green beans, jasmine rice, marinated black beans, quinoa, salad mix, etc.

There are so many meals I can create here. Now think about what you have in your freezer. Why is it there? There's this little thing called rotation. Make a list of everything in there and start using them one by one. A great idea for meals and simple recipes for you to create would be delicious soups, veggie burgers, stews, a stir-fry, and more. A potluck "night in" full of apps (aka leftovers) will work too! I freeze everything. Even my almond milk. I have now created recycled iced cubes that I just throw back in my juice or protein shakes. Same goes for fruit or veggies prepped. I make a soup or smoothie with them right away. Same flavor and no waste.

If you are unsure of what to create with what you have, please be sure to check out my recipes here and, of course, substitute with what you have on hand. Be creative in this process. If you're not in the market or really just want to save yourself time and not become the next best chef, then make a dump soup. It's all how you look at things. Whether you are throwing all the ingredients in a pot and hope it tastes okay or really want to put in the effort and create something amazing; how it will always start is in your mind. Mindset is everything, and how you look at what you need to accomplish is how you get the best results.

Let's recap here…

Plan ahead, prepare the night before, wake up earlier, make your list, use what you have, and get organized. Put alarms on your phone if you need them and put yourself first so that you can be the best for those around you.

CHAPTER TWO

PUT IN THE WORK

This is probably the most important part of the book. Know your worth. Visualize who you want to become. Create everything you want that doesn't currently exist. Follow those dreams, finish that DIY project, launch that course, better your family, and mend that relationship. Produce that podcast and build that brand. These are just a few things I've been able to accomplish over the last few years that if I hadn't chosen to put in the work, they never would have happened.

You absolutely must put in the work. This is why I set you up at the beginning of this book with the tools and routines to help you get this party started. The first thing you really need to take care of is figuring out what it is you really want. These are the hard questions you must ask yourself. There are a lot of people who have recently had to figure this out because of the pandemic and the pivots of life and business that had to happen. Luckily for me, my business and podcast were already online. However, that doesn't mean I didn't have a hard time. That doesn't mean I didn't make changes. I made huge changes.

One of them being this book. Another, the way I look at each day given to me. How I keep my mind from racing a mile a minute, how I don't get food delivered to me every day because I fell into such a deep depression and slump. Days I was afraid to even get out of bed. Thanks, COVID.

The last thing I wanted to do was create all these healthy recipes you see here in this book. I know I sound like such a hypocrite, but this is real life and mine that I have decided to share with you. If I didn't put in the work to get my head right first and foremost, there is no way in hell I would be sitting here on the beach writing this book. Life is tough. Let's just try to make it a little easier on ourselves. Little by little, you will find your way. It's trial and error, and honestly, I feel like that's the best part. It took me forever to find meditations that I liked. You know you really need to like the voice. I've realized years later that I love a good five to ten-minute meditation, and it's the 30 to 45-minute sound baths that really do the trick for me. Mental health is so important to talk about and something I've always been 100% open and honest about. I've shared how alone I felt, how the darkness became my home for a very long time, and how I was able to see the light again. To be completely transparent, there were days I never saw that light glistening in the distance. There were also days I didn't want to see it. Days I did wish that I would not wake up, and that is why I know that when you put in the work and create great things, anything is possible. I am alive and writing this book today, and I am genuinely happy again.

If you have never had to deal with mental health issues, I am so glad, but now that you've read a little bit more about mine, you will know how to react if someone close to you is going through a dark time. Be supportive and let them know that you will always be there for them, no matter what happens.

Work smarter, not harder. How many times have you heard that? If you listen to me throughout this entire book, I am giving you the tools and sharing everything that has worked for me. The best things in life will come easily to you because you have learned how to get yourself organized, your head straight, and you know what you want. You have a list; you have goals and priorities.

More importantly, you now have a purpose. Whether it's for yourself or your family and friends, you want to do what's right. You want to have a life filled with freedom and all the things you love, and the only way to get there is to save yourself some time, money, and energy. Get up earlier, begin your day with your own gratitude practice, and don't forget to make your bed. This, hands down, has been the key to my success thus far.

Make your schedule and menus the night before and watch everything you've wanted to create just come pouring in. When you set a goal and don't achieve it, for example, your recipe fails, you didn't land that job, or that deal didn't go through, please know that it is happening for a reason. It's setting you up for something even better.

I've had so many things fall through and not work out for me, personally and professionally. You have to just stop and ask yourself. Why me? I worked so hard, I prepared, I manifested, I did all the things.

Why the hell didn't this go my way? The only response I have for you is that everything happens for a reason. We may find out now, later or maybe never have an answer for the shit we have to deal with in our lives, but please know that from my very own experiences, it will all work out in the end.

Whether it taught us lessons we needed, made us stronger, more confident individuals, there was and is a reason, and better things will come your way because you've put in the work. Also, do you see a pattern here? Repetition and the formation of habits are key to your success.

RECIPES-BREAKFAST

GOOD MORNING GREEN JUICE

- Kale
- Celery
- Apple
- Orange
- Ginger
- Carrot
- Turmeric
- Cayenne Pepper
- Cilantro
- Apple Cider Vinegar

All fruits and veggies should already be cut up and prepped. If not, just take a few pieces of each to fill up your blending cup ¾ of the way.

Blend with green tea when needed.

If you are not a lover of kale, simply replace it with spinach and/or your favorite vegetables and without the spice.

CHUNKY MONKEY OVERNIGHT OATS

- ½ cup Gluten-Free Oats
- 2 tbsp Almond Butter
- ½ Gluten Free-Sugar Free Baking Cocoa
- ½ Banana
- 1 tbsp Chia Seeds
- ¾ cup Almond Milk
- 1 tiny little drop Vanilla Liquid Stevia. This sweetener is potent!

Other flavors to try are a peanut butter/chocolate, pumpkin nut, blueberry, or apple cinnamon.

Add everything in one mason jar the night before and enjoy for up to two days.

THE BEST ALMOND MILK

- 1 cup Almonds
- 3 cups Water

Soak for 24 hours. Blend with fresh water until completely liquified. Milk will be steaming once blended. Perfect time to add to hot coffee.

Add a tiny little drop of vanilla liquid stevia and a couple shakes of cinnamon for flavor. Pumpkin spice is also delicious.

This makes a lot of milk. ½ cup of almonds lasts me a week when adding to just my coffee.

Blend in two separate batches to get a smooth texture. Cheese cloth is not necessary, but you can use one if needed.

Use half the amount of water for a creamier texture.

Additional flavor option would be black sesame cashew milk.

PERFECT PROTEIN BARS

- 2 cups Gluten-Free Oats
- ½ cup Almond Butter
- ½ Almond Milk
- 2 scoops Vanilla Protein
- 1 tbsp Honey
- 1 tbsp Coconut Oil

Blend all ingredients in bowl and place into a square casserole dish. The wider the dish, the thinner the bars.

Freeze for about 30 minutes and then cut and wrap individually to grab on the go.

Additional ingredient options would be shredded coconut, dried fruit, dark chocolate, chia seeds, fig marmalade, pumpkin seeds, and walnuts.

You can also roll the dough into balls rather than placing them in a dish.

CHAPTER THREE

ENJOY THE LITTLE THINGS

Life is hard. Really effing hard. As I sit here writing this book for you, I realize truly how grateful I am to have this life and share these lessons and recipes with you. I've had more than a handful of moments in my life where it was a life or death situation.

Holding my breath, saying a prayer, and hoping for the best. It was those times when I came out of them that really made me realize that it was time to stop sweating the small stuff and start enjoying the little things.

It may seem odd that a personal development book and cookbook have come together, but it's honestly the only way to tell this story in full. The only way I've found my happiness and desire to help even more in this world is by writing this book.

I've always felt a strong pull in all paths I have taken in life thus far. It all makes complete sense because it's led me to this place of writing to you today. A couple of months ago, I decided to go on a neighborhood stroll and support a few small businesses, as we all know they need it. I went into the cutest little store and came across lighting fixtures, furniture, jewelry, succulents, gift cards, and kitchen gadgets, among other things.

When I was ready to leave the store, something told me to do another lap. Maybe I missed something? Well, I turned the corner and came across these sleek looking pencils. I asked the owner why she was selling them. We'll just file that under shit I ask random strangers. I'm always curious about the products and business aspects. Why are the pencils so amazing? Her answer was that she saw them at a convention, and they had a story. That they do. They have quite the cult following. Turns out these pencils were what I needed to write my story in this book for you today. I didn't know why I was trying to walk around the store again, but now I do.

I was typing out these chapters for a while, but it wasn't working out for me. The universe led me to these pencils. These incredible and mighty two-dollar pencils. To say I'm enjoying these powerful writing instruments would be a complete understatement. By the way, the whole reason for that neighborhood walk was to support another small business because I was out of my favorite incense.

Over the last two years, I've ventured into the more spiritual aspect of life. Higher powers, vibrations, believing, manifesting, visualizing, leaning in, feeling emotions, and more. I want you to sit down, take a moment, and write down what you're currently enjoying. You know all the little things. This practice is harder than you think.

Some of mine are lighting a match for my candle in the morning, the birds chirping before the rest of the world is up (I sometimes enjoy a 4:30 am wakeup), pouring cold water and slicing a lemon, making my ice coffee, listening to the silence when I wake up early. The sound of the waves crashing, watching the birds visit my window in the morning, the white noise of my fans because San Diego has been so hot this summer, the water boiling for my favorite jasmine rice.

The sound of the ice cubes hitting my glass in the morning for coffee, my friends laughing when I tell them I own a glue gun and DIY my walls for my video backdrops. When I share the latest ingredients from an epic market I've come across. When I make a meal with them, and it epically fails. See, I never said I was perfect. No way, no how could I ever be perfect. If you think you are, then I suggest putting this book down and investing in a self-help book or therapist and then coming back to me. These are just a sampling of the little things that make me smile. Now make your list and enjoy them to a whole new level because you deserve that happiness.

CHAPTER FOUR

EMBRACE THE CHANGE

I've always been one to be able to adapt very quickly. I didn't move around a lot as a child, but as an adult at least 50 times. Are you one of those people who can set up shop immediately when you travel? You arrive to your hotel, and you must unpack everything, like you live there. You need all your clothes hung up, office situation set up and products placed in the bathroom just the way you like them, as if you were at home. What about when you've moved? Do you relax and take time to unpack and figure out the best layout or immediately dive in headfirst?

For some people, this is hard, and for others, it comes so naturally. I am luckily one of those. I must wake up the next morning with a new vibe, clean, and organized space. This chapter is about how to embrace the emotions that come with change. I've always been a crier. Happy times, sad times, when I'm watching a rom-com, even over a great meal. Although that time is usually once a month. Wink.

Over the last few years, my emotions have been on another level. I mean, for sure 100% from all the drugs some awful doctors put me on. If you want that whole story, you can tune into my podcast at any time. Then out of nowhere, I went numb. I had zero emotions. Again, I will blame the drugs for that. Then about six months ago, I just started crying again. I mean, for no reason. I would start bawling. This is around the same time the pandemic started. Any song, TV show, even if they were laughing, it would make me cry. I couldn't control it, so I decided to embrace it; I mean, I was locked up in my house anyway. Writing this book brought up more emotions than I ever could have expected. I have literally cried while writing each chapter.

My therapist, who I speak to weekly (thank God for her), told me it's all part of the healing process. Something that I've been hearing so much more of lately is that you have to feel to heal. Oh my God, let me tell you how healing this book writing has been for me. I had no idea how different I would feel after getting everything from my head to paper. I know my gift is to share all of this with you, and there is a purpose so bear with me. I am feeling now; let's just get that straight right now. I have all the feels, if not more. It's next level if you ask me! Lol.

How do I embrace my emotions and change? When it comes to feeling, I used to be the worst. If someone would upset me, I would immediately cut them off. That's what I saw a lot of growing up, so I just assumed that was the way. Thank God I grew up and realized that is not the correct way to deal with life. Also, so grateful for those humans I cut off that are still my friends to this day. Get a group of friends you know will keep you in check. I'm forever grateful for them.

Throughout this journey we call life, bad things happen, great things happen, and we get thrown curveballs daily. Seriously, is someone upstairs trying to test us? Doesn't it always seem that when you have a million things on your plate, that is when you have to stop for a minute because a bomb dropped into the mix? We need to know how to embrace the changes and know how to pivot, learn from the current situation, and realign ourselves when it is over with. I do this all the time, and I'm sure you had to do it once or twice during the pandemic.

This shit is hard. Emotions are hard. But I promise, in the end, it will always make you stronger. I know this because I've been able to do it myself. Instead of being angry at the world, annoyed and anxious, try to switch your mindset to something like this. I needed a break to reevaluate my current situation and see my new everyday world in a different light. It's when these things happen to us that allows us to truly become the best versions of ourselves. Now I'm going to share what I do when my recipes don't work out. Everything is trial and error. Okay, let's talk about baking for a minute. I am not a baker. Well, minus my traditional yearly Irish soda bread recipe. Why do you think I have so many no-bake desserts in this book? I can make a mean stir-fry, but when it comes to measurements and all that shit, I simply don't have the patience.

Welcome to common sense cooking. It really is the best way to create in the kitchen. I knew I needed to challenge myself for this book, so I embraced the scary change and made it happen. It's trial and error, but sometimes the best meals happen that way, and I have quite a few of them sprinkled throughout this book for you. Trying to perfect a gluten-free self-rising vegan pizza dough I knew would be a challenge for me. I wanted to create a super healthy dough option for us busy people, but also have everything done in 20 minutes. The dough I'm happy to say I perfected on the first try. But when it came to my pretzels, gnocchi, and freezing it, it did not work out.

I embraced the change, learned from it, and made my current situation the best it could possibly be. Could I have stopped after my two failed attempts and be angry? Absolutely, but I knew that there was a reason for this happening. To share it with you here in this book. Life is funny, isn't it? I could have chosen one way to go with my mind, but I put it in the work, was grateful for the experience, fixed my mind, and made things the best they could be for myself, for you, and, of course the food. So happy to share after many attempts, all my recipes have been confirmed by my taste testers to be delicious. Embrace all the change, feel the emotions (as I am crying and typing), and good things will happen.

RECIPES-LUNCH

DETOX GARDEN SOUP

- ½ -1 cup Salsa
- Splash of Olive Oil
- 4-6 stalks Celery
- Handful Shredded Carrots
- ½ bunch Cilantro
- 1 Onion
- ¼ cup Garlic
- Parsley
- Kale
- Turmeric
- Cayenne Pepper
- Dill
- Oregano
- Handful Sprouts
- Handful Shredded Cabbage mix
- Lemon/Lime Juice
- Pink Himalayan Salt
- Black Pepper
- 1 Bay Leaf

Depending on how big your soup pot is and how vast your taste buds are, you may modify the number of vegetables and only add a pinch of the pepper and, of course, your favorite amount of seasonings.

Sauté olive oil, onion, and garlic first in the pot. This will give you more of a roasted flavor. Then add in all your other vegetables and broth. Just cut and put the ingredients into a pot. Super simple and quick! Add water ¾ to top of pot and less for a heartier soup.

Your broth will consist of water. Therefore, I use salsa to flavor. You can also add a vegan chicken seasoning or more salsa to flavor the water.

Bring to a boil and simmer with lid on for 30-40 minutes.

This is a great base of a soup to add vegan matzo balls, white navy beans, or jasmine rice to create more of a dense meal.

BUTTERNUT SQUASH SOUP

- 1 box Butternut Squash Soup
- Splash of Olive Oil
- Touch of Sesame Oil
- 1 Onion
- ¼ cup Garlic
- Pink Himalayan Salt
- Black Pepper
- Oregano
- 1 can Peas
- ¼ bunch Cilantro
- 3-4 stalks Celery
- ¼ bunch Parsley
- 2 Bay Leaves
- Handful Shredded Carrots
- 1/4 cup Pumpkin Seeds
- Turmeric
- Cumin
- Rosemary

Use olive oil and/or sesame oil to sauté onion and garlic first for fuller flavor. Add box of soup and fill up with water and then add salsa to flavor the water.

Next, add all the vegetables and spices.

Boil and simmer with lid on for 30-40 minutes.

Add garbanzo beans, black rice, or quinoa for a heartier flavor. I usually have these on the side, so it doesn't consume all the broth over the course of a few days while in the fridge.

GLUTEN-FREE PASTA SALAD

- 1 box Pasta
- 1 Red Pepper
- Handful Shredded Carrots
- 1 can Corn
- 1 can Peas
- ¼ cup Olive Oil
- ¼ cup White Balsamic Vinegar
- Pink Salt
- Black Pepper
- Oregano
- Dill

Cook one box of pasta and wait for it to cool off before adding in vegetables. I like to use a variation of two smaller pastas. Looks great for parties and your photos!

Prep all vegetables. Once pasta is cooled off, add in olive oil and all vegetables and balsamic vinegar. Mix so that the rainbow of your veggies starts to appear.

Add in all your favorite spices and place in the fridge for 30 minutes, so flavors adhere to pasta.

Serve and enjoy. The longer time in fridge, the richer the taste.

Additional flavor options would be to add ranch flavoring, Italian dressing, sugar snap peas with sesame oil, lemon, and basil.

LENTIL STEW

- 1 ½ cup Dried Lentils
- Splash of Olive Oil
- 1 Onion
- 3-4 tbsp Garlic
- 3 stalks of Celery
- Paprika
- Cumin
- 1 Tomato
- 1 small can Tomato Paste
- ½ cup Tahini
- Handful Shredded Carrots
- 1 Bay Leaf
- Cayenne Pepper
- Dill
- Pink Himalayan Salt
- Black Pepper
- Oregano

Use olive oil to sauté onion and garlic first for fuller flavor. Add in all ingredients that have already been chopped and fill to top with water. Add in all spices.

When I want more of a creamier flavor, I use tahini rather than tomato paste. For a thinner consistency, add more water.

Bring to a boil and simmer for 30 minutes. This is a very hearty soup.

CHAPTER FIVE

TAKE CONTROL

By now, you know that you have the power to control your thoughts. You have the power to make good choices and not so good choices. Here is a great example. Last night, I thought that I deserved some fried chicken. So, I downloaded a delivery app for the 100th time. I made a promise to myself no more deliveries, by the way.

I have an entire fridge and freezer full of healthy fruits and veggies and meal preps. I spent money on healthy foods, but for some reason, that little voice in my head said to order some fried foods. It was Saturday, and this store is closed on Sunday. You deserve that special treat. I had my order sitting in my cart for an hour as I watched some rom-com movies. And ladies and gents, I chose that I would have control over this situation.

I also reminded myself that I've been working out so hard lately. Why am I doing going to eat fried chicken at a time like this? I deserve more. I deserve better. I deserve to have complete control. I will. How? I made myself some super delicious air popcorn, which, by the way, is one of my all-time favorite snacks. I won. I won the game. My mind was racing, and I was exhausted, so this situation could have gone south. The possibilities are endless, but you must always have the control to power through.

We have control, and we can choose our destiny and can make anything happen. Manifesting and visualization are two things that I have incorporated into my life over the past four years, affirmations as well. I have a whole chapter on visualizations coming up for you, so right now, I just want to explain my experiences with manifesting more out of your life.

Just in case you're not familiar with manifesting, it is when something is put into your physical reality through thought, feelings, and beliefs. This means that whatever you focus on is what you are bringing into your reality, per the search engines. I told you, your mind is incredibly powerful.

I've manifested almost all of my dream jobs. Usually, the way that it happens is I wake up and want something more. I journal it out, create affirmations around it, and make it happen. I put my thoughts out into the universe and wait for everything to align. While that is happening, I am putting in the work, doing the research just to be prepared and acting as if it is already here because I know it is on its way.

I know it sounds like this is a little crazy, but honestly, I started doing this over ten years ago; before anybody was even talking about manifesting anything. What I am sharing with you now has always been my process. I mean, it all started out on my to-do list, and once you are on there, you may not leave until you are checked off. Kind of like an old school way of manifesting. If I want something, I write it down and go out and get it. I will always find a way.

Some things will be harder than others, but those are what we call little life lessons. Finding and having solutions has been a pastime of mine. Although, I never realized until a client pointed that out to me a few years ago. I was like, *Oh my God, you are right*, but you see, I never looked at things that way. I always just had a to-do list and knew what projects and what work had to be done and just figured it out. I have had so many situations in my personal life and career where I would have only a few minutes to figure out a solution. Literally minutes. In a normal world, some would allow days to find an answer, but when you work in luxury travel with the elite, you are in a whole new world. A demanding one, but one that always keeps you on your toes, challenges you and your mind to extremes you never thought possible. I am so grateful for those experiences. I could also write an entire book on that part of my life as I am now out of all my NDA's. I just don't think anyone would even believe it. Oh, the stories I could tell...

Again, the mind is so damn powerful. Now let's use it the right way to control our new destiny.

CHAPTER SIX

THE POSSIBILITIES ARE ENDLESS

We're halfway through, friends...

The possibilities will always be endless. However, you must have the right mindset and just allow things to happen. I've had to let go of so many emotions, feelings, relationships, and more over the last few years. And that was so hard for me. I have had to sacrifice so much to get me to where I am right now. That is just what needs to happen. I am still sacrificing. It is worth it to me because it will pay off in the end and get me to that next best chapter of my life where I need to be so I can continue to help others.

I'm not about to sugarcoat anything for you because I want you to see all sides. Feel all sides because this is how you will become the best version of yourself. Do we see a pattern here? We are all living in a much different world right now. Large corporations are closing, pivoting, and shifting their business model and allowing their employees to work from home. More companies are introducing wellness and mental health options in their programs. Seriously though, it's about time...

They're finally realizing how important these factors are when it comes to productivity. If you have had to pivot, design a new work area at home (home school vibes), and just try to survive through this new chaos and still feeling frustrated and unorganized, please know you will find a solution for it all. Adjusting to create your new normal is what everyone is trying to figure out right now, so don't let the stress get to you, okay?

Creating a business or shifting the one that you have online will never come easy. It may come naturally but never easy. You may be part of a direct sales company that hands you everything you need for your back office, but it is your job to go out and get the business.

You rely on social media and platforms that you do not own. That is scary! You know what you do own? An email list! If you are not currently using an email marketing automation service, I highly recommend you do so today. By the way, if you are not on my email list to receive my weekly newsletters, head to my website, and join today. Wink. I want to be crystal clear with you for a second. You do not need to have a business for the need of an email list. These will also come in handy when it comes time to send holiday cards. Digital cards are the best because you will save time, money, and energy without having to stop at the post office. These cards can be sent immediately or scheduled, so you are able to send on time. You'll also save a tree.

The possibilities are endless when it comes to creating a business, home project, or new family plan. If you are someone like me who loves creating things and helping people, then here is your subtle little nudge to let you know that it is time to start that business or organizational project you've been dreaming about. I am a prime example that you can start an online business with no investment. Granted, some businesses will need at least a couple hundred, but there are always ways around that, and you can start when you're ready. Sometimes diving in headfirst works too! Raising my hand over here...

I started my podcast without any big investment. I recorded over one hundred episodes on my phone, downloaded production software, purchased a domain for one dollar, and got my first month free for my hosting platform. After that, it jumped into $12.00 a month. After I launched my podcast, I was approached by many other business professionals and coaches in the online space, asking me how I launched my show. As always, I saw the need to create something that needed to exist. I needed to design a platform that would allow others to share their own personal stories or brand messages.

I created and launched a Done For You boutique podcasting service. I also had some coaching options available for those that wanted to learn and felt comfortable with the technical side. Can we just have a moment of silence for a minute for the fact that I taught myself how to produce podcasts? I mean, don't go asking me hard-hitting questions because I still don't even know what to call the work I do. I just know what buttons to press and make my show and all my clients sound incredible.

Okay, so now that we're clear on that, honestly, I just had to give myself a pat on the back because seriously, how did I do that? See the trend here? Anything is possible. I used to paint faces, serve on yachts, and book charter planes for a living. I am the queen of making shit happen, and you may also hold that title, but you didn't know it until now.

I want to now share with you how I grew this program so fast without a marketing budget. Referrals. My business is 100% referrals. Once I launched the first few podcasts of my clients, I knew I had something great, and they did too because they sent their friends and colleagues to me. I wanted to put something together to thank them, so I launched an affiliate program. If I needed to post about the program, I would always share my reviews. I pride myself on my service and reviews. Trust me, you can see them for yourself on my website and podcast. Rather than pay a social media platform for ads, I offered a commission to my clients as they were the first ones to start sharing and tagging me all over the Internet.

I absolutely loved the podcasting process. Writing scripts, designing the website, coaching them on the market, sending music options, pitching brands, executing notes, and syndicating their shows. That is my absolute favorite part. Helping their dream become a reality, having their message heard. Showing them how to build their brand and get in front of a global audience. That right there is an endless possibility.

Podcasting is the medium I chose to share my story to help others. I had no idea what I was doing, but I heard Gary Vaynerchuck's voice in my head saying, *just fucking do it*, so I did it. Podcasting changed my life. Podcasting saved my life, expanded my thoughts, and empowered me to create more and a change for others. The possibilities are endless with podcasting as well as anything in life. You must be willing to create an opportunity for yourself to have them in your own life and be sure to manifest that shit now.

Onto the food aspect. When writing a cookbook, the possibilities are endless. I mean, I have been creating recipes for decades. But when it came time to put them together, that was tough. How do I categorize this book? How do I not pigeon hole myself? How do I finalize everything from years of concocting recipes? I spent hours online just trying to organize everything. That was one of my favorite pandemic pastimes.

After years of writing, I finally made the decision to stop talking about my traumatic personal stories. I decided this book needed to be about the happy times in life. Write about what you know. Make the readers think, act, smile, and laugh. So, I pivoted and decided to write my cookbook. After all, the kitchen is where I am the happiest, and creating meals can literally be fun for the family, or just you. We all need that "me" time.

I was absolutely thrilled and enjoyed this process, but the book was missing something. It did not feel like it was 100% me. I realized something that was missing was my stories. I cannot just share my recipes; I need to share my stories of how I got to this place in my life that I am currently living in. How I got here was a shit ton of personal development. There will be stories that are happy, maybe a bit sad, hilarious because we know by now my life has never been normal.

This is how this book was born. As far as the recipes, just as in the chapters to help you uplevel your life, I am starting with the basics. Keeping it simple. My mission is not to stress you out but to show you how to enjoy the process and your life, because it is time!

I thought it was easiest and best to give you the best in basic recipes. Super healthy meals with no meat, no dairy, no gluten, and no added sugar. Of course, you can add them in at any time. When I mention or when you feel like being creative. Live on the edge. It's time! Try making your own and see what happens. I have messed up so many times. I am in no way 100% Vegan; I just enjoy eating good healthy meals, and sharing them with you makes me so happy as the possibilities are truly endless.

THE MOST DELICIOUS QUINOA SALAD

- One bag of shredded Cabbage or Broccoli Slaw
- 2 cups cooked Quinoa
- 1 can Butter Beans/White Navy
- 1 cup Rice Vinegar
- 1 Zucchini
- Lime Juice
- 1 Onion
- ¼ cup Garlic
- ½ bunch Cilantro
- Maldon Salt
- Red Pepper
- Olive Oil
- Sumac
- Dill

Cook quinoa. Put it in the fridge with olive oil to chill.

Add all cut and prepped ingredients and spices to a large bowl. Add in quinoa. I prefer a small dicing of the veggies.

Chill in the fridge for 30-45 minutes. Add more lime juice, stir, and serve. The longer in fridge, the zestier the flavor.

Additional flavor options would be pineapple and mint, avocado and jalapeno, corn, and peppers for a more southwestern flavor.

Butter beans will create more of a creamier salad rather than the navy beans, or you could always use a little bit of both.

MANDARIN VEGETABLE STIR-FRY

- Touch of Sesame Oil
- Splash of Olive Oil
- Tri-colored Peppers
- 1 bag Green beans/Broccoli or both
- 1 can Water Chestnuts
- 1 can Baby Corns
- ¼ cup Minced Garlic
- ½ Onion
- 1 bag Beans Sprouts
- 1 can Mandarin Oranges
- Lime Juice
- ½ bag Okra
- Pink Himalayan Salt
- Red Pepper
- Scallions for garnish or add more in stir-fry for flavor.
- Black Sesame Seeds

I use a can or bag of each vegetable to make enough for the week to meal prep.

In a large skillet on medium heat, sauté all vegetables over olive oil, garlic, and onion. Add in salt and pepper here.

Once halfway cooked, add in sesame oil, spices, mandarin oranges, and black sesame seeds on cook on medium/high for 5-10 minutes until nice and crisp.

Serve over jasmine rice or rice noodles, add your favorite sauce, and garnish with cashews or peanuts.

VEGGIE BURGERS FOR THE WIN

- Peas
- Corn
- Handful Shredded Carrots
- Olive Oil
- Garbanzo Beans
- Sunflower Seeds
- Salsa
- Pink Himalayan Salt
- Sumac
- Dill
- Turmeric
- Cayenne Pepper
- Minced Onion/Garlic
- Onion Powder/Garlic Powder
- Oregano

I use all canned vegetables and beans for the recipe. Fresh and frozen create a softer consistency. Trust me, the cans work so much better.

After washing and straining out all liquid from the cans, add ingredients into a large bowl and mix. Next, blend in Cuisinart. You will need to do this 3-4 times because of the amount you are blending. Smaller batches work best. If you blend everything at once, the texture of the burgers will be off.

Have another bowl ready for the blended ingredients. Once you are done blending your batches, add in your oil, salsa, and spices. Mix everything up.

The consistency of this should be sticky but not too wet from the salsa. If it does get to thin where you cannot form a burger patty, just add in some gluten-free breadcrumbs or a binder like lentils or quinoa. More sunflower seeds may just do the trick!

Spray cookie sheet and then portion out 1/3 cup burger patties. Molding in the fridge or freezer for 30 minutes helps form the burger. This recipe will make you at least a dozen burgers.

Sautee both sides of the burger in a skillet and then bake in the oven for 30 minutes on 350 degrees. Use the broiler for a crispier texture.

Additional flavor options for this recipe would be adding black beans with sweet potato or lentils with cumin seasoning.

MARGHERITA PIZZA

- 1 Tomato
- Minced Onion
- Minced Garlic
- Pink Himalayan Salt
- Maldon Salt
- Black Pepper
- Oregano
- Fresh Basil
- Vegan Mozzarella Cheese
- Balsamic Glaze
- Nutritional Yeast/Sunflower Seeds for crust

HOW TO MAKE SELF-RISING GLUTEN-FREE FLOUR

- 4 cups Flour
- 2 tbsp Baking Powder
- 2 tsp Kosher Salt

Mix ingredients in bowl and save in air-tight container.

HOW TO MAKE PIZZA DOUGH

- 1 ¾ cup Self-Rising, Gluten-Free Flour
- 1 cup Non-Dairy Greek or Cashew Plain Yogurt

Blend in a bowl until good sticky consistency. Add olive oil to smooth out the dough and leave in the fridge for 10 minutes. Flipping dough after five minutes.

Once the dough is ready to go, roll out over the pizza stone. Cover the top of the pizza with olive oil, garlic, and tomato slices. Next, add on all the other toppings and spices minus the cheese. As much as you desire. As for the crust, I like to add sunflower seeds or nutritional yeast and maldon salt for flavor.

Cook for 25 minutes at 425 degrees and add cheese and oregano halfway through cooking time. I like to broil for five minutes. Garnish with balsamic glaze drizzled over the pizza.

Additional flavor options for pizza are BBQ mashed potatoes, caramelized onion, and vegan ricotta cheese or a white pizza with ricotta, mozzarella, and garlic, no tomatoes.

CHAPTER SEVEN

YOU DESERVE THE BEST

As I mentioned earlier, I have always prided myself on providing the best service. I'm guessing that came from working in the restaurant industry at such a young age. I've always had guests, customers, clients, vendors, and colleagues that I was always determined to go above and beyond for. I want all of them to be happy with my work, and I truly do love just helping people.

I mean, I am a perfectionist, so that too. But honestly, I've always loved to work even at an early age. Creating and serving just always made me happy. Hence the name of my podcast and brand. So why is it that we tell ourselves this crazy story that we don't deserve the best? I'm here to tell you that no matter where you are in life, you absolutely deserve everything you have been putting on your vision board.

Manifesting, visualizing, working so damn hard for. We also deserve to experience the best service, although some just don't know how that works. If you are in a service-based business and maybe not trained properly, it is not your fault, but you do have common sense, right? I'm not saying this to be mean; I'm just stating facts that work so that you can take them and run with it and be the best version of yourself. First, I want to share with you why you need to experience the best.

Do it for yourself first. Take the time to make yourself a nice meal. Take out that never used china, drink your iced coffee out of an extra-large size mason jar (that's me). Pour your sparkling water in a champagne glass, create a five-star spa experience for yourself. Bath salts, skincare fridge, heated towels, etc.

Why don't I deserve to be pampered with a mid-day bubble bath, while the oil diffuser is pumping out eucalyptus, and my mood lighting of red or lavender is setting the true tone? I mean, you really need to go all out. When I go out, I love when someone greets me immediately. Hello, that is just manners. I mean, even with a mask on. It's nice to hear. You deserve little things like this as well. You work hard, right? So, you deserve to create a new story for yourself. One that allows you this time to indulge.

Now, if you're going to tell me there is no time in your day for this, I'm going to remind you that we have 24 hours in a day. Wake up earlier. I have a big deadline with this book. Do you want to know how I'm getting it done? I wake up earlier and sacrifice time with friends. Second, if you are someone in the business of serving (don't kill me but even if it's for your family), go above and beyond. We're all tired at some point or another. Obviously, you know when it's time to take a break. You'll feel it; you'll get moody and irritable, so I suggest you take one as needed. That's my prescription for you...

Going above and beyond just feels good. Spend a few extra minutes laughing with your friends or family. Send them a signal that shows them how much you appreciate them. When it comes to business, I want to share a few service and etiquette tips that I always use. Now before I get into them all, I'm fully aware we can all have a shitty day;

we are human. Those are the days you smile and nod and just keep your mouth shut, you know, so you don't offend anyone.

If you are not interested in the business aspect, no worries because these tips can be implemented into your daily life as well. You can also share them with a friend or family member who may need to see them or maybe even the girl at your local drive-through where you visit every single Sunday and still does not greet you by name. Telling them about this book would be a great service.

Greet others by name and provide your service with a genuine smile and upbeat personality. Nobody wants to work with a negative Nancy. Go above and beyond, answer questions in a timely manner. Offer an upsell, have legit manners, always always follow up, thank them for the business, and always ask for a review. I could go on and on, but I do not want this to turn into a business book, so maybe that will be my next one.

What is one thing you deserve right now? Don't be greedy; just be grateful and start small. Enjoy the process of now allowing yourself the time to experience this because you effing deserve it, especially after surviving a pandemic. Insert a certain female rapper's version of saying okay! Just to make this point clear!

CHAPTER EIGHT

FUCK THE FEAR

I've always been somewhat of a fearless person, and the thought never even crossed my mind to actually write about fear because when you read these chapters, you kind of get that through my words. However, I just got a little reminder on my phone that three years ago, I was sitting in a chemo chair for my fifth treatment.

I used to watch videos of the ocean waves crash repeatedly, visualizing that I would one day make it back to the beach. No more ports and picc lines, no more drugs, no more relapses. Just me on the beach. Being my old happy, healthy version of myself. Again, that was a sign I had to write about being fearless. I'm literally sitting here living the life I thought I would never get back. If you are someone who needs a little push from someone, I'm your girl. I'm definitely not a daredevil or an adventure thrill seeker. I'm not into scary shit or heights. Fuck the fear, make a list of shit you need to make happen, and do it. You only live once. I got my life back, so I know and feel that it's my duty to help you become fearless.

How I got through chemo, a misdiagnosis, six legal cases, and a list of other stressful life events was the fact that I was fearless. I was also absolutely petrified of dying, although I knew that was always an option. I know, deserve, and expect more, and I know that you do too. What are you afraid of? Make a list and tackle them one at a time. Don't try to be an overachiever here; it's just too much. Trust me, I've already tried. Start by asking yourself why you are afraid. Journal that shit out and meditate on it. I mean, try hypnosis if that helps. If you have the answers, then it's easier to get over, as I mentioned earlier.

There is something so magical about putting pen (in my case, pencil) to paper. If there wasn't, then I would not be doing double the work for myself to write this book. I would have just audio recorded it and dictated it all. I wanted to face my own fears about writing this book. Can I do it? Is anybody going to read it? Why would they buy my book and not someone else's with a bigger following and notoriety? Are they going to think this two in one book idea is insane?

I worked hard on my thoughts, meditated, answered my questions mentioned above, and made this book happen. Everyone has a story to share, and this is mine. Everyone has unique gifts to offer to the world, and this is mine. Life lessons, advice, and delicious healthy recipes. It's good to be scared, have a challenge. It helps us personally grow and become better versions of ourselves. Fearless!

I looked at my chemo treatments as a job, and ten years before (again, not the norm) that I was taking care of someone who was going through the same thing. It was my job! So, I knew when it was my turn to act the same. I always had to fight for sanity and peace of mind all by myself. On those days, I would mentally have to convince myself that the drug getting dumped into my veins would not close my throat up in a matter of seconds and kill me because it could have at any given moment. I mean, it definitely tried…

My anxiety would be through the roof, and when I showed up, I would just be in full panic mode even after the drugs they gave me. I would have somehow convinced myself today would be my last day on Earth, and then I would start to visualize my funeral and see everyone who was there. I know that's super dark, but that's fear. My fear, my story, my truth, my darkness. I fought those fears, fought the thoughts, fought the drugs, and fought the doctors, and I won.

I won because I don't think like that anymore, thanks to years of therapy. I won because I'm not sick, and I won because I'm alive to share that story with you here from the very beach I used to dream of coming back to. I got the control back of my mind. Now, I'm here to help you face your fears. Again, if you don't have a cheerleader, I'm your girl. But you first must believe in yourself. I want you to know that you can be as fearless as you want. Baby steps are always okay…

I just want to remind you that I am only sharing my truth and the decisions I chose to make and the way I decided to fight to serve as inspiration and motivation for you to start your own process. They will always look different because we are different. Now it is time for you to say eff off fear. I am done with you. It is time to fight your own battles in your own way that feels right to you. In a way that you know in your heart and feel in your gut is right for you.

RECIPES-SAVORY SIDES

SALSA FOR DAYS

- 2 Tomatoes
- 1 Onion
- 2 tbsp minced Garlic
- 1 tbsp Olive Oil
- ½ bunch Cilantro
- 2 Limes for juice
- Pink Himalayan Salt
- Black Pepper
- Jalapeno Peppers for added heat

Blend all diced vegetables, herbs, and seasoning in a small blender, chill for 30 minutes and serve. Batch stays fresh for about a week.

Additional flavor options would be mango, peach, pineapple, black beans, and corn.

GARLIC AND HERB HUMMUS

- 1 can Garbanzo Beans
- 2 tbsp Olive Oil
- 4 tbsp minced Garlic
- ¼ cup Lemon Juice
- 2 tbsp Tahini
- Sumac
- Dill
- Pink Himalayan Salt
- Black Pepper

Wash beans and drain out liquid. Place all ingredients and seasonings in the blender on medium. Use a spatula to clean sides in between blends.

Replacing garbanzo beans with butter beans will create a creamier texture.

If you do not have Tahini, you can use almond butter instead.

Additional flavor options would be basil and pesto, everything bagel seeds, roasted red pepper, and jalapeno lime.

SWEET AND SPICY BRUSSELS SPROUTS

- 1 bag of fresh, not frozen Brussels Sprouts
- Coat with Olive Oil
- Pink Himalayan Salt
- Red Pepper
- Oregano
- ¼ cup Minced Garlic
- 1-2 tbsp Honey
- Drizzle Balsamic Glaze

In a large bowl, add all ingredients together and layer over tinfoil covered cookie sheet. You can pan sear, but oven is best. I usually just cut brussels sprouts in half.

Cook for 25 minutes on 425. Stir halfway through cooking time. I like to broil for a few minutes to give a real good crisp around the sprouts.

Additional flavor options would be sesame peanut and garlic parmesan.

SWEET POTATO FRIES

- 1 Sweet Potato
- Olive Oil
- Cinnamon
- Red Pepper
- Pink Himalayan Salt
- Oregano

One potato makes 3-4 side portions. Cut up potato in strips, rounds, or squares. Place in large bowl and coat with olive oil and seasonings. I place in a plastic bag and leave in the fridge for a few hours or for a full day to marinate.

Place on olive oil sprayed tinfoil cookie sheet and cook for 25 minutes on 425. You can also cook on medium/high in cast iron skillet for additional charcoal flavor.

Additional flavor options would be using coconut oil for a sweeter taste and more onion, rosemary, and garlic for savory.

CHAPTER NINE

CREATE AND EXECUTE A PLAN

There are so many ways for you to save time, money, and energy. Let me get you all set up and organized. Whether you have a super tight budget or unlimited funds (I've had both), these steps will set you up for success and get you to that next step you deserve to be at. You know how I feel about planning, getting up early, and putting in the work. Be more productive with your scheduling. Plan your day, week, month, or even year out at a glance. This will save you time. I just briefly want to mention the power of a good high highlighting system. I've been using one for years, and I have strategically designated specific colors to map out and guide me through my days, weeks, months, and year.

They all have a meaning and responsibility to show me where I belong and at what time. I do a lot, as you, and so do you! The reason why I'm successful is because I know how to make shit happen. Get yourself organized number one. Plan with some time. Save your receipts and organize them in categories and per month. Do this with medical records, business, and household items as well. Execute a plan that you know you will stick to and one that will keep you on your toes and organized. I've been using this system for years. Again, envelopes and black marker available from your local dollar store. Also, if you have returns to do, following up with a doctor or looking for an older invoice, you can find what you are looking for in a much shorter period.

Planning a menu or meals in advance will save you a ton of money because you're not throwing random ingredients together in the fridge you are preparing in advance. I live in San Diego, one of the most expensive cities in the country. If I can buy $20 worth of fruits and vegetables to juice every morning for two weeks, you can too. Obviously, it is going to be a little bit more for a family, but you get what I am saying…

Groceries here are in abundance. I literally go to four different stores to get all the basics. Six, if you count my specialty items. By the way, the better foods, fruit, and veggies you eat, the more energy you'll have. If you plan a menu on the weekend for the upcoming week, just think about how much more time and energy you will have for your friends and family and/or business. I have a lot of delicious recipes that you can create and freeze. Yes, I'm a huge fan of the freezer and have simplified some good techniques.

Make extra meals per week and freeze so you don't get sick of the same thing every day, especially if you are meal prepping. When your homemade almond milk or fruit smoothies are sitting in the fridge about to go bad, freeze them into iced cubes and add them to your coffee and smoothies. When you buy all the veggies to juice and they are about to expire, create a delicious detox soup to clean you out. I am not a nutritionist; I'm just speaking from experience.

When you get your fruit and veggies home from the store, wash them and prep them right away. An excellent idea that will add more storage space to your fridge. When everything is already prepped, you'll have a fridge and freezer full of options. This really comes in handy on those busy days you want to eat an unhealthy snack or if you're a busy, on the go type of person. Portion out your snacks and meals in to-go containers.

If you've already put in the time and energy creating delicious options, please make sure to spend the time to organize your fridge, freezer, and pantry exactly how you want it. If you are the one doing all the cooking, then you are going to want everything you use daily easily accessible. Always have a running grocery list. Produce, dry goods, miscellaneous. Try to get everything at once and stock up. Again, saving you time, money, and energy. Have fun creating and designing the fridge that makes sense to you and/or your family. Please remember to just enjoy this overall process. If this isn't your cup of tea, then delegate someone else to do it and put your feet up and enjoy that tea! Wink.

I never buy enough where I cannot find it. I always need to see everything I have so that I can create meals with my "use what you have method." Once I knew I was going to be sharing recipes with you, I went to target and the dollar store to buy containers that I would need to hold all my new spices.

I have one for small spaces, large spices, and other pantry items. I'll organize some on my shelf and the rest is in my pantry in my room, as I shared with you earlier. If you ask me where everything is right now, I could tell you exactly. You should be able to do the same. If you have way too much, you need to start creating meals, soups, etc.

A serious fridge and freezer cleanout and organized pantry party should happen somewhere in your near future. Contact me, and I'll give you some tips. You know, I still have friends and clients that call me asking me where everything is in their pantry, office, and desktop I organized for them years ago. For some crazy reason, I always remember. I guess I'm pretty good at organizing and/or have a photographic memory.

Let's do another little recap, shall we?

Saving time will allow you to live without regret. We only have so much time here. Save money where you can so that you can indulge in something bigger. Cancel subscriptions you are not using and watch that money come back to you. Energy. We all need it. Eat healthy so that you can enjoy more of your life. Isn't that what we all want?

CHOCOLATE MINT ICE CREAM

- 4 Bananas
- ½ cup Baking Cocoa
- Fresh Mint Leaves or Peppermint Extract
- 1 tsp. Vanilla Extract
- ½ cup Almond Milk

Cut up bananas. Place all ingredients and blend on medium until the texture is creamy. If using a smaller blender, this will be 3-4 small batches.

Freeze overnight. I recommend using iced cube trays, popsicle sticks, or small bowls to portion out. Makes a good pudding if left in fridge, if you don't prefer the frozen consistency.

Additional flavor options would be to add peanut or almond butter to replace mint or pumpkin, cinnamon, and nutmeg for a festive flavor. I like shredded coconut with the chocolate as well!

FRUIT SORBET

- Assorted variety of cut-up Fruit.

Add to blender. Add almond or coconut milk for thicker smoothie consistency. For a thinner consistency, blend with green tea.

Freeze overnight. I recommend using iced cube trays, popsicle sticks, or small bowls to portion out.

I like to use the frozen sorbet cubes in my smoothies to create a thicker consistency.

CHOCOLATE DESSERT HUMMUS

- 1 can Black Beans
- ½ cup Baking Cocoa
- 1 tsp Honey
- 1 tsp Cinnamon
- 1 tsp Vanilla Extract or a tiny drop of Vanilla Liquid Stevia

Blend all ingredients on medium until thick texture. Place in the fridge for 30 minutes. Garnish with strawberry, serve, and enjoy.

If using a smaller blender, this will be 3-4 small batches. Add more Tahini for a thicker texture and more water to thin it out.

If you add some coconut oil, you can turn this hummus into no-bake double cholate truffles. Just roll out the dough-like consistency.

PUMPKIN OATMEAL COOKIES

- 1 can Pumpkin
- 2 ½ cups Gluten-Free Oats
- 2-3 tbsp Honey
- 1 tsp Cinnamon
- 1 tsp Pumpkin Pie Spice

Mix all ingredients in a large bowl. Roll into 1-2 tbsp sized balls. The consistency of batter will be quite sticky so keep an olive oil spray and small spoon next to you for your hands.

Cook on 350 for 10-15 minutes.

Additional ingredients to add for flavor would be dark chocolate, walnuts, shredded coconut (1/4 cup), and nutmeg. I love to grate dark chocolate chunks in batter.

CHAPTER TEN

ACCEPT WHO YOU

The honest truth hurts, but guess what? You were put on this planet for a reason. To be a good person, to do good work, and help others. Now there are a million ways for you to do this, and so that is why it is so important for you to find your true purpose in life. And it can most definitely be more than one, and it is always good to try things out. You never know until you try…

Don't expect anything from anyone. We all have dreams and ways we plan on chasing. We get creative, we make a plan, and we go after them in our own way. So why is it that when we tell the people around us about them, they cannot understand? They cannot support in the way that you expected.

Maybe they will tell you that there is no way you can do it. That it doesn't make sense. Logistically or financially. They don't believe in dreaming or you to dream at all. They believe in waking up day after day living the same routine.

I am here to tell you that none of that matters. These are your dreams, and no one else's. Your dreams are yours for a reason. That reason being it is you that can handle them and truly make them a reality. You know you will put in the work, and you know those negative voices around you could not handle the work. So, stop thinking about them and dwelling on the bad stuff and focus on the good.

When it comes time to chase those dreams, start that family, build that brand, create that community or launch that business, I want you to do it because YOU want it and not for anyone else. You cannot make someone else's dreams a reality. They must be your own.

Stop scrolling and spending time on social media. Stay in your lane and focus on your results. Stop looking to see who is watching your stories on social media. Stop expecting people to like and comment on all your posts. This may make you feel sad that your inner circle doesn't give you all the love, but everyone is busy, just like you. Especially now, while homeschooling 2.0 is happening.

I cannot tell you how many people come into my inbox to mention one of my posts but never like or comment. Clearly, they don't know how online business owners need the algorithm to work in their favor. It is okay because the greater the content you put out into the universe is, the more people who really need to see it will. Don't be offended like my old self.

Don't focus on the negative; focus on the positive. The fact that you get to wake up every morning, do what you love, create amazing things throughout the day, and turn those dreams into a reality.

This is your dream to chase. So now go and do just that. Go out and get the happy, healthy, positive, and productive life you so deserve…

EPILOGUE

I wrote this book because I wanted to share my stories with you. Real-life shit that will make you feel like you are not alone and empower you and to know that you can do anything. I wanted to write messages that would hit home, that would give you another perspective, that would give you the courage to become fearless, more productive, healthier, and organized so that you can have the life you truly deserve.

I wanted to remind you that anything is possible, and the opportunities are endless. However, you must put in the work to get the results that you want.

Your mind and thoughts are so powerful. Mental health is important. So always make sure you are taking care of yourself first before anyone else. This matters the most.

Tap into your intuition. We are living in quite a different world right now, and if you feel that it is time to make some moves, just effing go for it! There is no one or nothing that can possibly hold you back. You are the only one who could get in your own way. And you know that now.

If you are anything like me, then you know that you deserve more, but at the same time, you want to do more for others. Get a journal and just start writing. Start manifesting what it is that will truly set your soul on fire. Visualize it happening and then start acting as if it's already here.

You must do the work, mentally, physically, emotionally, and spiritually for all of this to happen the way you've been dreaming about, so now is the time to start.

Be efficient. Start saving time, money, and energy by implementing the steps I spoke about earlier.

Use what you have. Follow directions. Do something amazing. Get creative. Make healthy choices in all aspects of your life. If that job or friend is no longer serving you, then it is time to move on. Thank them for the experiences and lessons and grow from it. Move on...

Begin each day with gratitude, stay humble, grateful from the moment you open your eyes, and start a new morning and evening routine that will help you become the absolute best version of yourself.

You deserve to live a happy, healthy, positive, and productive life. I hope this book gave you the tools and confidence to go out and get what is yours. A life that you truly love and most definitely deserve.

Thank you for investing in this book and yourself. Thank you for reading it in full. Thank you for allowing me to share my truth, my recipes, and my heart and soul with you. This was indeed an adventure, and I am so glad I put my own mind and tools to work so that I could complete my very first book for you.

Thank you for laughing at me and with me, and thank yourself for giving yourself this time to learn, grow, and do more. Thank you for following my recipes and putting your own spin on them. With your food and your life...

If you enjoyed our time together, I would love it if you would share this book with someone you know who needs it in their life right now. And as always, I would appreciate a review from where you purchased this book. This allows my message to be seen by others who may really need this book in their life, and at the same time, you are doing good work, providing a service to others so that they can do the same. I am always available online, so please do not hesitate to tag me and reach out through any messenger.

Until next time...

DON'T QUIT

WHEN THINGS GO WRONG AS THEY SOMETIMES WILL,

WHEN THE ROAD YOU'RE TRUDGING SEEMS ALL UP HILL,

WHEN THE FUNDS ARE LOW AND THE DEBTS ARE HIGH

AND YOU WANT TO SMILE,

BUT YOU HAVE TO SIGH,

WHEN CARE IS PRESSING YOU DOWN A BIT,

REST, IF YOU MUST, BUT DON'T YOU QUIT.

LIFE IS QUEER WITH ITS TWISTS AND TURNS,

AS EVERYONE OF US SOMETIMES LEARNS,

AND MANY A FAILURE TURNS ABOUT

WHEN HE MIGHT HAVE WON

HAD HE STUCK IT OUT;

DON'T GIVE UP THOUGH THE PACE

SEEMS SLOW-

YOU MAY SUCCEED WITH ANOTHER BLOW.

SUCCESS IS FAILURE TURNED

INSIDE OUT-

THE SILVER TINT OF THE CLOUDS

OF DOUBT,

AND YOU NEVER CAN TELL

HOW CLOSE YOU ARE,

IT MAY BE NEAR WHEN IT SEEMS SO FAR;

SO STICK TO THE FIGHT WHEN

YOU'RE THE HARDEST HIT-

IT'S WHEN THINGS SEEM WORST

THAT YOU MUST NOT QUIT.

— JOHN GREENLEAF WHITTIER

ABOUT THE AUTHOR

Kelly helps business owners organize their space, build momentum, stay accountable, launch successful podcasts and most importantly enjoy their life.

She teaches the power of visualization; mindset shifts and how to manifest more by calming your mind with a holistic approach.

At an early age it was clear to people around Kelly that she was destined for a career using her outgoing personality and creativity.

With a true passion for color she started off painting which led to photography and then blossomed into a love of makeup artistry and design.

Since starting her beauty, luxury, business and service driven careers, Kelly has traveled to the most exotic and remote locations in the world, whether on a cruise ship giving seminars to cooking, cleaning, wining and dining on board private yachts and jets working with the elite.

From folding napkins to curling lashes Kelly has seen it, done it and strives to do more! After years of working for corporate America,

Kelly realized something was always standing in the way of her true connection to the client.

That something was the corporations. She realized that a personal relationship was needed, a direct connection to Kelly!

In 2016 Kelly was diagnosed with MS and in 2017 she was diagnosed with an extremely rare autoimmune disease called NMO. She quickly learned that becoming an advocate for your own health and rights would be a full-time job and knew she needed to use her voice and create a platform for others to come to, be heard and learn more.

That is when The Happy Workaholic Podcast was born. A show focused on Business, LinkedIn and Life with an Autoimmune Disease. Three things Kelly knew best!

In 2019 Kelly found out that she was misdiagnosed with both diseases. Not only did she have to change her way of every day thinking and living life she also had to change the format and model of the show.

The new and upgraded version of The Happy Workaholic Podcast is intended to elevate your mind, upgrade your business, enhance your life and become a part of a positive and uplifting community.

Inspiration, motivation, determination and a never give up attitude are what got Kelly to where she is today, and she cannot wait to share the stories of other inspirational entrepreneurs, professional patients, healers, business owners and fellow podcasters who will be featured on the show.

Kelly has always taken a more personal approach to business. She continuously uses her expertise and knowledge to raise awareness through patient advocacy and grow The Happy Workaholic Podcast, Network, A Million Dreams Publishing, her coaching experiences, and consulting programs she has created in order to enhance your business and life and get you to that next level you deserve to be at!

For the latest in business, life, podcasting and publishing news visit thehappyworkaholic.com.

RESOURCES

EVERYTHING IS MESSY

Storefront-Pantry Products

Kitchen Appliances-Community

everythingismessy.com

amilliondreamspublishing.com

CONNECT WITH KELLY

Website and Coaching Programs: thehappyworkaholic.com

Podcast: thehappyworkaholicpodcast.com

Facebook: @thehappyworkaholic

Instagram: @thehappyworkaholic

LinkedIn: @kellyanngorman

Twitter: @kellyanngorman

Pinterest: @kellyanngorman

YouTube: @kellyanngorman

Medium: @kellyanngorman